Say "hello" to B

Big Boy is an

Alaska Sled Dog Puppy

Alaska Sled Dog Puppy Coloring Book

Dedicated to Tapestry and Homer, two very good dogs.

Ridge Rock Press • SAN #253-6595 • P.O. Box 255 • Healy, Alaska 99743

Gina Soltis and Lori Yanuchi, authors. Wendy Bown, illustration and design.
Printed in the United States of America
ISBN 0-9670177-1-8
Job #50002499
May 2014

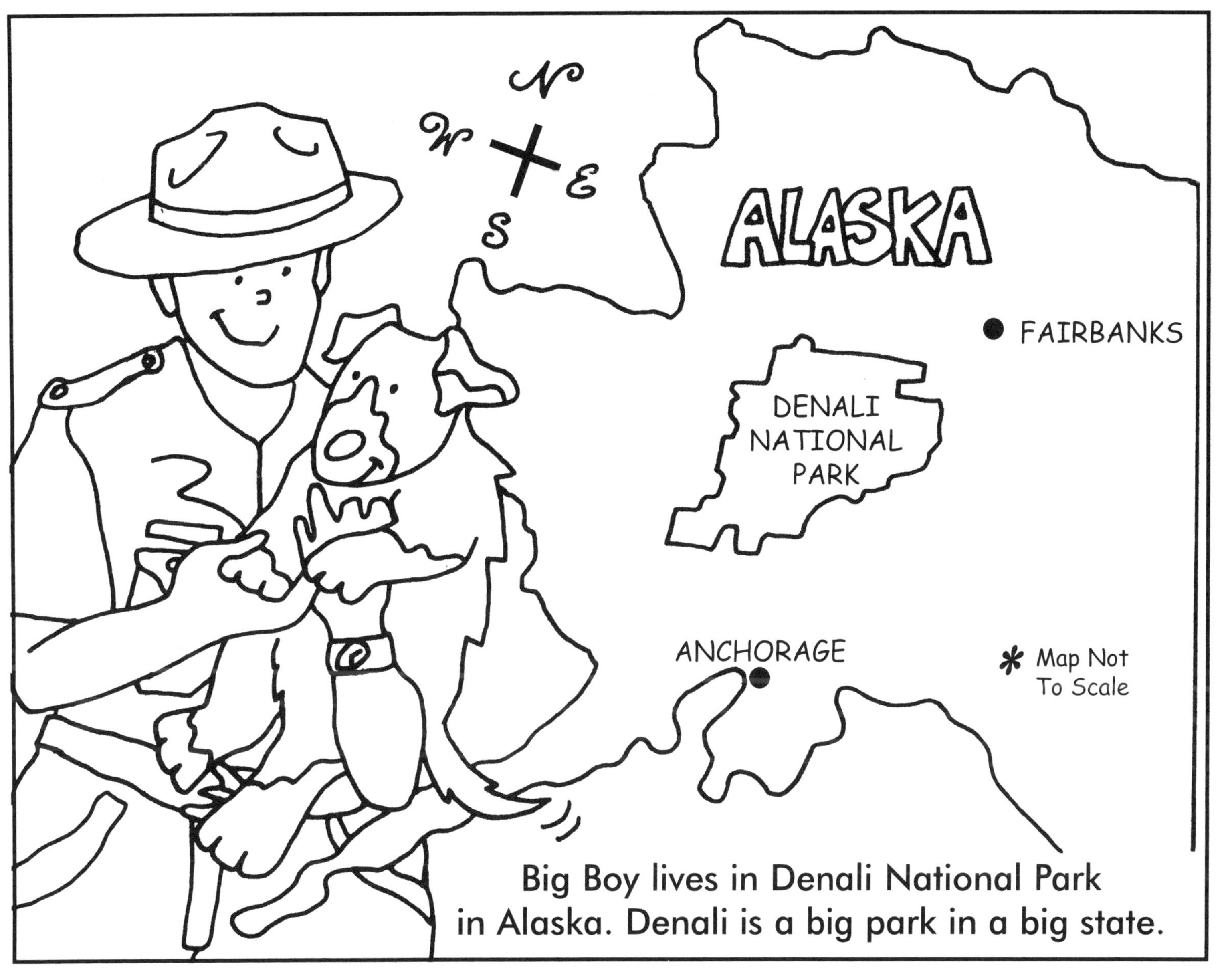

Big Boy lives in Denali National Park in Alaska. Denali is a big park in a big state.

Big Boy was born at the kennels in Denali National Park. He and his litter mates are huskies, bred to be sled dogs - strong, fast and smart.

Their heavy coats keep them warm in the winter.
Their big paws help them run fast over the snow.

A person who runs sled dogs is a musher. The park ranger musher hitches the grown up dogs to a dog sled. Big Boy's mom is in the front position. She is the lead dog.

Each dog is put in a harness which is connected to a line that pulls the sled. When all the dogs are hitched to the sled they are called a sled dog team.

The musher says "gee" and the dogs turn right.
He says "haw" and they turn left. "Whoa" and the whole team stops.

Big Boy and the other pups are young so they don't yet pull the sled. They run along side and learn by watching the older dogs.

WE
LOVE TO RUN!
IT'S FUN,FUN,
FUN!

After the run, it's time for a rest. The ranger gives the sled dogs their food and water and the playful pups are fed too.

These hard working dogs eat very good food and drink plenty of clean water.

The rangers love mushing with the eager sled dogs.
They reward the dogs with love and yummy food treats.

The rangers are patient when they are teaching the puppies.
A gentle scolding is all the pups need when they make a mistake.
They get lots of praise when they are good.

To keep the dogs healthy, they are given shots and pills from the veterinarian. Whenever a dog looks sick, he is given immediate care.

I TAKE
MY VACCINE
SO I'LL BE STRONG
FOR MY TEAM

Good food and lots of exercise help keep the
sled dogs healthy and happy.

During the summer many people from all over the world come to see the sled dogs of Denali National Park.
PUPS
I WON'T BE SHY IF YOU COME SAY HI

At the sled dog demonstration the rangers and dogs show how much they love working together.

Today Big Boy and the other dogs say "good bye"
to Big Boy's aunt Pitka.
AAWOOOO
GOOD-BYE
AUNT PITKA!
ENJOY YOUR NEW
HOME IN SITKA!

When a Denali sled dog is too old to run in a team, he or she is adopted by a nice family and moves into their home.

Work is done, play is done. It's time to go to bed. Each dog sleeps in a warm, dry dog house on a snug bed of straw.

Big Boy likes being a sled dog puppy at Denali National Park in Alaska.
He hopes you can come visit.

Alaska Sled Dog Puppy Coloring Book
Word List

Sled Dog - A dog trained to pull a sled.

Dog Sled - A special sled that is pulled by dogs.

Dog Team - The trained group of dogs that pull the sled.

Lead Dog - A smart dog who is up front in a dog team.

Mush - To drive a dog team.

Musher - A dog sled driver who gives commands to the lead dog. and the dog team.

Husky - A dog bred to be a sled dog.

Kennels - A dog home with dog houses.

Veterinarian - An animal doctor.

National Park - A special place to visit, to see beautiful scenery and wildlife and to learn history.

Park Ranger - A person who works at a national park.

Sled Dog Demonstration - A summer program at Denali National Park which shows how a dog team works in the park during the winter. A dog team is hooked up to a sled on wheels and run on a gravel track.

Mushing Commands given by the musher to the dog team

"hike" means "go"
"gee" means "turn right"
"haw" means "turn left"
"whoa" means "stop"

To learn more about the sled dogs of Denali
visit the Denali National Park Kennels web site at:
www.nps.gov/dena
and click on "KENNELS"

Running with the Big Dogs
A Sled Dog Puppy Grows Up In Denali National Park, Alaska
by Lori Yanuchi and Wendy Brown

A full color story book that invites children to mush along with the sled dogs of Denali. Share the wonder of a puppy as you follow him through his first year of adventure and learning. 32 pages. ISBN 0-9670177-0-X

Alaska Sled Dog Puppy Coloring Book
For younger children. Learn about the daily life of a sled dog puppy. Bring the story to life with color. 24 pages. ISBN 0-9670177-1-8

ORDER FORM

Name:	
Address:	
Phone:	
Credit Card #:	
Expiration Date:	Visa, Mastercard or Discover
Signature:	

COUNT	TITLE	PRICE	TOTAL
	Running with the Big Dogs	$8.95	
	Alaska Sled Dog Puppy Coloring Book	$4.95	
	Shipping		$3.50
	TOTAL		

Mail to: Ridge Rock Press • P.O. Box 255 • Healy, Alaska 99743
Fax orders to: (907) 683-7737